CW00330198

DOOMSDAY

A SURVIVAL

HANDBOOK

DOOMSDAY: A SURVIVAL HANDBOOK

An exclusive edition for

for all your gift books and gift stationery

This edition first published in Great Britain in 2020

Allsorted Ltd, Watford, Herts, UK WD19 4BG

© Susanna Geoghegan Gift Publishing

Author: Magnus Allan

Cover design: Milestone Creative

Contents design: Bag of Badgers Ltd

ISBN: 978-1-912295-18-0

Printed in China

10 9 8 7 6 5 4 3 2 1

DOOMSDAY

A SURVIVAL
HANDBOOK

Doomsday is near;
die all, die merrily.

William Shakespeare

CONTENTS

Introduction _____ 7

Categories of the Apocalypse _____ 10

Doomsday Scenario #1: The Mad Scientist _____ 16

Doomsday Scenario #2: The Supervolcano _____ 19

The Phases of Doom _____ 21

Doomsday Scenario #3: War of the Worlds _____ 32

Doomsday Scenario #4: The Plague of Vampires _____ 35

The Bug-out Bag _____ 38

Doomsday Scenario #5: Sun Boils Over _____ 40

Doomsday Scenario #6: Grumpy Vegan Plants of Doom __ 42

Torch or Head-torch? _____ 44

Doomsday Scenario #7: Supervirus _____ 48

Doomsday Scenario #8: Nuclear War _____ 50

The Importance of Having a Hobby _____ 53

Doomsday Scenario #9: Reactor Meltdown _____ 72

Doomsday Scenario #10: Impact Event _____ 74

What to do if you Missed the Alarm and Slept
Through the Apocalypse _____ 77

Doomsday Scenario #11: Coronal Mass Ejection _____ 84

Prophesies of Doom _____ 87

Doomsday Scenario #12: Financial Crisis _____ 89

Reading the Writing on the Wall _____ 91

Doomsday Scenario #13: Feline Overlords _____ 94

Conclusion _____ 95

Don't wake me for the end of
the world unless it has very
good special effects.

Roger Zelazny

INTRODUCTION

We live on a fragile lump of rock floating in the vast emptiness of space. One of our nearest neighbours is a gigantic ball of burning plasma, a self-perpetuating thermonuclear explosion that's more than 100 times bigger than our planet. Our understanding of the sun is improving every day, but there's still every chance that it could do something unexpected. And unexpected is unlikely to be good for us.

The void around our planet is filled with spinning space rocks on erratic orbits. Space is dark, the rocks are dark, and everything is dancing around the sun at incredible speeds. If a big rock happens to stumble into our path and bump into us, it would probably be a real crimp on our week. Or our millennium.

Then there's the chance that a civilisation on a distant planet has developed a way of zipping around the galaxy and has decided to pop in for a visit. Maybe they are after new conscripts for their galactic war. Maybe they need hosts. Maybe we're their trail snacks.

Basically, it's not safe out there.

But then, it's not massively safe down here either. There are mutating viruses; there are supervolcanoes; there's the possibility that the myths and legends of our various cultures could turn out to have an element of truth. What if a breed of vampires rises? What if they already walk among us?

And this is before we get into the possibility that we could be the architects of our own destruction. History has shown that we are quite capable of handing over power to megalomaniacs, and our love affair with technology often has surprising consequences.

We are surrounded by danger, but that shouldn't stop us living our lives. We simply need to understand the risks, take precautions, and learn when not to investigate that strange noise in the cellar during a storm with a torch that's literally on the blink.

That's where this book comes in.

We are going to look at 13 possible apocalypses, assessing them for feasibility, impact and survivability.

DANGER: WAR OF THE WORLDS

DANGER: THE SUN BOILS OVER

DANGER: IMPACT EVENT

DANGER: REACTOR MELTDOWN

DANGER: CORONAL MASS EJECTION

DANGER: THE MAD SCIENTIST

DANGER: PLAGUE OF VAMPIRES

DANGER: FELINE OVERLORDS

DANGER: GRUMPY VEGAN PLANTS OF DOOM

DANGER: SUPERVIRUS

DANGER: FINANCIAL CRISIS

DANGER: SUPERVOLCANOES

DANGER: NUCLEAR WAR

CATEGORIES OF THE APOCALYPSE

There are many ways that the world we enjoy today could draw to a close. Some are simply irritating and disruptive; some distinctly fiery and destructive. It is difficult to draw a line between where one category ends and the next begins, but broadly perhaps it is useful to try and picture an apocalypse on a spectrum of potential society-altering calamities.

Everything's normal. Bing-bong, you just received some spam email. Reassuring, isn't it.

For your consideration, take the example of the mobile phone and its potential to unleash five different levels of catastrophe.

CATEGORY I

It would be a bit of a hassle if our phones stopped updating and all our precious apps stopped working.[*] We'd have to change the way that we shopped, which for some would be a kind of apocalypse.[†] The long-term ramifications for society might not be significant, but it would probably take us five years to build the infrastructure we'd need to move back from our smart phones to our parents' dumb phones.

Phones and apps are not updating.

---

[*] An app-ocalypse, perhaps.

[†] Going to the supermarket would stop being an occasional novelty and return to being a weekly chore that everyone would have to endure.

CATEGORY II

If our mobile phones stopped working entirely, the implications would be more concerning. Not only would it be more difficult to talk on the phone, emails would become less simple to send because we'd have to go back to desktop computers, and we'd have to start actually using our brains to remember people's birthdays. Banks and post offices might have to start reopening and we'd need to learn to queue again. We'd also have to relearn how to read maps. And carry cameras and buy photo albums. And music. And address books. Perhaps it's still more irritating than apocalyptic, but it seems fair to say that it would represent a 10- to 20-year setback to the global economy. Some would win, many would lose.

Phones are not working at all.

CATEGORY III

If our phones spontaneously exploded, the loss of life could be significant. Walk down the street in any town or city and probably one in ten people will have a phone glued to their ear; many more have their phones in their hands as they study maps and read information. The rest tend to have a phone in one of their pockets, safely tucked away near their vital organs. Beyond the psychological scarring that the survivors would endure, the sudden loss of trust in technology would probably cause significant damage to society. Teenagers

All phones explode.

would be forced to find new ways to avoid interacting with people properly. At best, you are looking at a 30-year setback for the world.

CATEGORY IV

But then, what if, instead of exploding, phones went actively bad? What if this vast global communication network achieved some sort of sentience and decided that it was time to wipe the scourge of humanity from the face of the earth? Even if we won, fighting the war and rooting out the influence of the mobile phone could take more than half a century and involve untold losses.

Phones achieve sentience and make a bid for global power.

*The implications that this particular manoeuvre will have on their monthly data allowance are as yet unclear, although there are suggestions that it is already accounted for in the small print of many contracts.

CATEGORY V

Finally, there is the true apocalypse, where the phones, having achieved sentience, discover a way to move beyond their fragile plastic and glass shells and ascend to a higher plane of existence, becoming beings of unlimited potential that exist in a quantum realm

Phones tear a hole in the fabric of space–time as they transcend this physical realm.

that is far beyond human understanding.[*] They ascend, perhaps without malice, but also without looking back, and as they leave they do permanent and irreparable damage to the very fabric of our reality, shattering our understanding of time and space. That is your Category V apocalypse, ladies and gentlemen, and there's no coming back from it.

So, as you can see, there are many ways that the apocalypse could go down, and the end of the world means different things to different people. Understanding what is happening is the first step to possible survival.

DOOMSDAY SCENARIO #1

THE MAD SCIENTIST

According to many glorious Hollywood movies through the years, the world is chock-full of slightly deranged scientists who are beavering away on their Ultimate Doomsday Devices (UDDs). The best of these troublemakers have a genuine grievance against the world, although many appear to do it for no other reason than they were bored on a rainy Tuesday afternoon and wanted to give a square-jawed hero or sassy heroine* something to quip about.

In reality, the reason why a mad scientist has not yet managed to complete their UDD[†] comes down to simple economics: UDDs tend to be expensive to build, power and maintain, and very few people around the world have the sort of resources necessary to get one up and running without seeking external investment.

As anyone with a small business knows it can be difficult to attract investment without a comprehensive business plan, and

---

[*]You can tell the difference: a male hero will tend to wear a tuxedo and be standing square to the camera looking stoic, while a female heroine will be clad in impractically tight leather and implausibly high heels and be looking whimsically or even coquettishly over her shoulder at the camera in publicity shots. Nobody knows why this is, as a well-cut tuxedo should also look great from behind.

[†]So far as we know...

comprehensive business plans that involve the end of the world have two major drawbacks. Primarily, they often attract the attention of square-jawed heroes or sassy heroines[Σ]. Secondly, from a venture capital point of view, a doomsday-based business plan struggles to offer long-term returns as a result of limited economic activity post-apocalypse.

Planning permission can also be a significant restraint.

It may come as a surprise to politicians at both ends of the spectrum, but perhaps it's our managed free-market economy coupled with a well-balanced bureaucratic structure that keeps the mad scientists lurking in their lairs in the craters of extinct volcanoes.

THREAT LEVEL:

[Σ]Or the people in the back-office that tend to do all the real work but rarely find themselves on movie posters even when they could wear a tuxedo with élan and have mentioned to the director that they would be more than willing to stand square-on to camera looking stoic or with their back to the camera looking whimsically over their shoulder in impractically tight leather and implausibly high heels. Just saying.

DOOMSDAY SCENARIO #2

THE SUPERVOLCANO

Before a mad scientist can set up a lair in an extinct volcano, there needs to be a volcano. Normal volcanos can be a bit of a hassle. When Eyjafjallajökull[*] erupted in 2010, it messed up international air travel for days, mainly because the wind direction took the ash that spewed out straight over Europe, making it dangerous for airlines to fly[†]. Around 10 million journeys are thought to have been disrupted.

[*] Pronounced: I'vehadaneyeful.

[†] At the very least, imagine what flying through a storm of pulverised pumice will do to the transparency of a windscreen at 350 mph.

19

This was a short-term challenge but hardly apocalyptic. The thing is, though, that the 2010 Eyjafjallajökull eruption was rated as a category four on the Volcanic Explosivity Index (VEI), ejecting less than 0.1 cubic kilometres of volcanic material into the air.

When Vesuvius erupted in 79AD, not only were the towns of Pompeii and Herculaneum wiped from the map, it was severe enough to be mentioned by the very few active historians of the age. It was a VEI-5 event, with less than 1 km^3 of volcanic material thrown into the air.

There is evidence of around 40 VEI-8 events taking place during the geologically recent history of the planet. These are thought to pump at least 1,000 km^3 of hot ash, super-heated tephra and other material into the atmosphere, blotting out the sun and causing crop failures, famines, diseases, mini-ice ages and other unpleasantness.

The eruption of a supervolcano would test our ingenuity as a species to its limits, and the fact that there hasn't been one for around 74,000 years would suggest that we are probably due one soon. That rumbling from Yellowstone may be more than just a hungry bear's stomach.

THREAT LEVEL:

THE PHASES OF DOOM

If you are lucky enough to be enjoying a Category I, II or III apocalypse, the chances are that the end of your world will happen in relative slow motion. There are likely to be five distinct phases, and you'll need different strategies to cope with each. Meanwhile, in the background, if the media's still working, there will be lots of people trying to divert the blame onto someone else ...

CRIKEY! WHAT'S THAT? RUN IN TERROR

When the history of doomsday is written,[*] the first phase will become known as "the dark times". During this period, most people find themselves to be quite busy doing three things simultaneously:

[*] This is a book full of optimism, of course someone will survive to write a history book. What were you expecting?

1. Trying desperately to work out what has happened
2. Trying desperately to work out how to stop what has happened happening again, more so, or to anyone else
3. Running in terror[*]

There might still be information coming out from official sources during this period. Whether this information is reliable or simply officials trying to pass the blame onto someone else on the off-chance that they survive and need some deniability will be anybody's guess.

This is clearly not the responsibility of the corporations, we simply created the packaging for the box, it was those fools in the in the media that opened it ...

NEWS

Latest: Local man reports bad moon rising, sees trouble up ahead... Doo

Either way, it's probably a sideshow. You need to focus on working out how to get through the next few days.

While this will not be the time for philosophy, if we were going to give it a philosophical name it would be chaos. Something will go wrong, this will have ramifications, those ramifications will lead to challenges, the challenges will evolve into problems and the problems will mount up to become a catastrophe. And once you reach catastrophe, it's possible that everything will stop working.

SURVIVAL TIP

If anything is happening that seems a bit odd, such as flashes on the horizon or that nice Mr. Smith from down the road suddenly turning a little bit bitey, move in the opposite direction. With extreme purpose.

OKAY, WE'VE GOT OUR HEADS ROUND THIS, THE VEHICLES ARE STILL WORKING AND THERE IS STILL CANNED STUFF IN THE SHOPS

In the aftermath of the catastrophe, there is likely to be a period where things return to some sort of equilibrium. Cars might still work and if you are lucky enough to find yourself somewhere near a supermarket or food distribution warehouse of some sort, there could well be some pre-apocalypse food around. Make the most of your favourite sweets, crisps and craft beer, the expiry date will come around soon.[†]

---

[*] Hopefully they'll have somewhere to run to, but at this stage that's not guaranteed.

[†] Even if you lose track of the actual date in all the excitement. If it's turned green, don't eat it. Unless it's a lime. In which case, sniff it first.

The big problem is that once there's been a catastrophe, the odds of a calamity being layered on top are significantly higher.

This is not a time for relaxation, this is a time for taking stock, working out what still works, what can be made to work again with a bit of ingenuity, and what is likely to be consigned to the world that was while you get on with surviving in the world that is.

I think we can all agree that the labelling on the box was far too small and as such the failure to register a warning should absolutely be laid at the government's door ...

NEWS

tor Strangelove suggests that we weren't actually supposed to open it...

SURVIVAL TIP

Hoard stuff. Fortify the food shops. Keep cars running for as long as you can. Be polite but don't trust anyone.

WELL DONE US, WE'VE RE-CREATED A PRE-INDUSTRIAL SOCIETY WITH SOME MODERN EMBELLISHMENTS, AND THE KIDS HAVE RECOVERED FROM THE END OF SOCIAL MEDIA

With any luck, you'll look back on this period with a smile. People will be dusting off recipe books and rediscovering

Blaming the government is clearly an outrageous failure to take responsibility on the part of the opposition. They committed to the box discovery programme during their disastrous term in office ...

NEWS

sident James Dale expected to address the nation live at 5pm... Local M

the simple joy of making ice cream without a freezer, birds will be singing in the trees* and people will be sharing their skills on a barter basis.

By this stage, you should have a fairly good idea about what caused the catastrophe and be able to make changes to the way things work to reduce the risk of it happening again. Builders and architects will be doing brisk business, but so will farmers, doctors, vets and members of the local yarn bombing society†.

From a philosophical perspective, there's a strong chance that a system of anarchy will evolve: a society with rules but without rulers.

----

* Assuming that your original catastrophe wasn't bird-based. It could happen. Don't trust them. It's only a few years since they dominated the Earth as dinosaurs, and it could be that they want their planet back. Have you noticed that they never look you in the eye?

† Who will be needed for clothing production and minor surgical procedures. You know the sort, you can find them in welcoming tea shops in every town. They bring their needles and tell yarns...

The problem with this approach is that most people will default back to the sofa given half a chance. Despite the inclement weather, people need to be working in the fields to get the harvest ready, protecting and rebuilding infrastructure as appropriate and making sure that everything's ready for winter.

We were in government at the time, but that's a very different thing to being in power. It was the universities that found the box and uncovered the incantations needed to open it ...

NEWS

ayor Richard Wilkins IV highlights potentially positive for aspects for loc

And to do that you are likely to need an executive committee that is willing to make decisions. And some of those decisions could be difficult, so maybe it's only fair that they move into the slightly bigger dwellings, get the pick of clothes that the local yarn bombing society are creating or the scavenging parties bring back. It's probably also fair that they get to skip the queue to have their plumbing seen to before anyone else if it looks like a problem might be developing.

SURVIVAL TIP

Summer doesn't last for ever, so make hay while the sun shines. Heal yourself and help those around you heal. Learn as many skills as you can.

> HUH, THE DIFFERING APPROACHES TO REBUILDING SOCIETY HAVE BROUGHT US INTO CONFLICT AND ALL THE PETROL/POWER CELLS/CHOCOLATE DIGESTIVES HAVE RUN OUT

At a certain point, there is a risk that these executive committees will start to evolve, and fiefdoms will arise. These will generally be led by charismatic people in slightly worn-out tuxedos.

Most of these fiefdoms will preach peace, proclaiming that they understand the lessons of the Dark Times. In ringing tones, they'll tell us how they will protect people from the risk of the Dark rising again. Ceremonies to celebrate life and ward off a second apocalypse will become common.[*]

As time goes on, the claim that the leadership understands the lessons of the Dark Times will imperceptibly transmogrify into a claim that they alone understand the lessons of the Dark Times. Protecting the people will change into protecting their people. It might be worth not asking too many questions too loudly in public, as if you look closely at the executive leadership team, you may notice that trusted lieutenants have started to disappear.

---

[*] Assuming that whatever caused the issue in the first place isn't attracted by torchlit processions and voices raised in praise.

This is hardly the time to play games and I think we owe it to the public to be honest and admit that it was the military that first proposed using the box ...

NEWS

al economies... Explorer George Taylor suggests we are all "Maniacs" in

There could be simple explanations: perhaps they have joined an important outreach program with another community a long way away, or it could be that they have made the brave decision to go and search for their lost dog in another county on the other side of the mountains. Either way, one day they'll be in the inner circle that leads the community, the next day they will be conspicuously absent.

At the same time, tensions between neighbouring communities of survivors will begin to be ratcheted up ...

SURVIVAL TIP

Remember where you stashed things, keep your bug-out bag stocked and handy. Learn all the highways and byways of your locality

SITTING ROUND A DYING FIRE TELLING OUR CHILDREN'S CHILDREN ABOUT THE WORLD THAT WAS

After the batteries have run out and the cars have stopped working, after the fiefdoms' incessant battles have led to their own collapse, after the vampires have all but won,[*] there will come a time when you will find yourself huddled around a fire telling stories of the world that was.

> Frankly, this is just typical beatnik nonsense. The unions were trying to tie us in so much red tape that we simply had to cut through it ...

NEWS

a heated press conference... British man claims that we should call him

You'll reminisce to your children's children about airports and football stadiums, traffic jams and hypermarkets; about the days when you could go to a drive-through restaurant and enjoy a burger that probably didn't contain any rat.

The children will look at you, their sad eyes dancing with disbelief and wonder, and the fire will burn low.

[*] All right, it's unlikely, but maybe vampires get a lucky win.

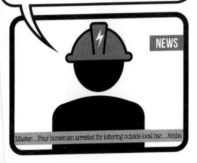

We warned those clowns that this was what would happen. They chose to carry on with that disastrous unboxing policy that went against our recommendations ...

NEWS

Master... Four horsemen arrested for loitering outside local bar... Amba

And you will keep talking, not because you need to remember the time before, not because you need to impart your knowledge before you are gone, not because if you stop the fire will be allowed to burn down and you will be left without warmth in a long, cold night.

No, you will keep talking because the alternative to talking is listening to that guy with the dreadlocks that has somehow, against all odds, managed to salvage an acoustic guitar from the decaying carcass of a fallen civilization.

He's always there, waiting in the shadows just beyond the fire's glow.

And he remembers some Ed Sheeran songs.

SURVIVAL TIP

I think we are a bit past that now aren't we?

WeLL, iT's hardly Likely To be our fauLT is iT, We are JusT here To bring joy To aLL The boys and girLs ... WhaT's ThaT you Say, iT Was a jack-in-The-box ...?

NEWS

ssador's son presented with new dog... Soylent Industries reports

It's the end of the world, we should all draw together, make the most of each other, and enjoy what little time we have left.

In the spirit of the end of the age, at the end of it all, the experts will stop shouting, stop pointing fingers, stop the blame game ... they will finally all agree on one thing. They will all agree that the best way forward is to form a bipartisan committee to carry out a comprehensive inquiry which will seek input from all relevant survivors and submit a preliminary report in three years' time.

As they come together and announce their intention, you'll notice flames breaking out in the background of the television studio. The picture will fade to black.

DOOMSDAY SCENARIO #3

WAR OF THE WORLDS

We don't yet know whether life exists beyond the comforting confines of our precious little blue and green planet. The balance of probability would suggest that it's probably out there in some form or another, but the important question from the point of view of an alien invasion is does *intelligent* life exist?

And if intelligent life exists, has it managed to avoid the many potential extinction level events that humanity has managed to sidestep so far?*

And if intelligent life exists and has shimmied past the many pitfalls that can face a civilization, has it developed a way of traveling faster than light to cover the almost incomprehensively vast distances of space?

And if intelligent life exists, has dodged its own mad scientists and the universe's selection of random events, and developed a way of circumventing intergalactic expanses in relatively short periods of time, will it actually be bothered to covert the Earth's bountiful resources?[†] Would they want to go through all the time and hassle it would take to rule over us?

---

[*] At time of writing.

[†] Five billion years on the clock, 10 billion careful(ish) owners.

There is an extensive range of factors that need to be met before aliens come knocking at our door asking politely if they can borrow a cup of sugar.[*]

That said, there is a risk of expansive intergalactic xenophobes coming to wipe us out, or less civilized alien societies that have inherited/acquired technology from long-extinct elder races who have come ravaging across the galaxy. So maybe it is worth keeping an eye on the heavens just in case those dust plumes recently witnessed in the Oort cloud turn out to be something more than just a naturally occurring event.[†]

THREAT LEVEL:

[*] While pointing a quantum-locked interphasic quad cannon at our icecaps.

[†] Please relax, no dust plumes have been witnessed in the Oort cloud. Mostly because the Oort cloud is still only theoretical because our telescopes are not yet powerful enough to confirm its actual existence, let alone offer the level of detail necessary to see the launch clouds of any individual intergalactic invasion craft that might be hidden within it. It's all fine. What you don't know probably can't hurt you …

DOOMSDAY SCENARIO #4

THE PLAGUE OF VAMPIRES

The popularity of amoral immortals with a hunger for haemoglobin tends to ebb and flow in popular media. They've come a long way from their folklore origins, and the stories that they are involved in can be good fun,[*] but you have to ask yourself one simple question: Why?

---

[*] Often depending on whether you like the square-jawed hero who is wearing the tux and whether you feel that the heroine's leather armour is too tight to be realistically practical.

What possible evolutionary niche does a nocturnal predator who can be defeated by a door actually fill? If a plague of vampires descended upon the world, we'd simply have to make really sure that we had enough milk in the fridge before sunset, remind ourselves not to answer the door, and then spend the hours of darkness enjoying a hot chocolate either in front of the TV or catching up on sleep.

With the right financial incentives, house builders would presumably rise to the challenge and add some sort of sealable front section to suburban houses so that if someone did come to the door begging for help in the middle of the night, you could let them into a comfortable porch area without giving them permission to enter the main house. They could wait out the night safely and comfortably. You could even leave out a camp bed for them if you were feeling particularly benign. Come the dawn, if they are still there then they are probably human. If not, this is your chance to dust the porch like you've been promising.

Sure, bars, clubs and restaurants might take a hit as a result of the lack of evening trade, but a plague of vampires would struggle to be a realistic catalyst for anything above a Category I apocalypse.

Of course, some kind of "science" experiment could go wrong and a breed of humans with an insatiable appetite for blood could be accidentally let loose upon the world, but the risks seem relatively low.[*]

THREAT LEVEL:

[*] See Doomsday scenario 1.

[†] Extra fangs awarded for their influence on popular culture.

THE BUG-OUT BAG

The bug-out bag (BOB) goes by several names, but broadly its purpose is to make sure you are ready in the event of anything over a Category II apocalypse. It is basically a bag, kept in a safe, easy-to-find place, filled with everything you need to survive the first three or so days of a major catastrophe. A bag that will give you a head start when trying to stay alive during the "Crikey! What's That? Run in Terror" phase of the end of the world.

BOBs have three major characteristics:

1. They are light (because you could well find yourself running in terror)

2. They are easy to find (because you will be in a hurry while running in terror)

3. They are kept up to date (because when you are running in terror, you need to keep your energy levels up and there's nothing worse than a stale protein bar)

As ever, it's hard to say what will help in the event of a specific type of apocalypse, and you can't carry something that covers every contingency. For example, you might need buoyancy aids in the case of a flood, raspberry yogurt in the event of werewolves, or something equally unexpected in the case of a black swan event.

To keep your BOB light, you need to focus primarily on common-sense pieces of BOB kit and then top it up with items as it becomes clearer how civilization is going to come crashing down.

THE BASIC BOB CHECKLIST

- ☐ 72-HOURS' LONG-LIFE FOOD
- ☐ 3 GALLONS OF WATER
- ☐ WATER-PURIFYING TABLETS
- ☐ HEAD-TORCH*
- ☐ FIRST-AID KIT
- ☐ DUCT TAPE
- ☐ BEDDING
- ☐ LOCAL MAP

- ☐ PONCHO
- ☐ FIRE-MAKING TOOL
- ☐ THERMAL EXPOSURE BLANKET
- ☐ MULTI-TOOL
- ☐ GLOW STICKS
- ☐ CASH
- ☐ COMPASS
- ☐ HAND SANITIZER

- ☐ MORE DUCT TAPE
- ☐ ID DOCUMENTATION AND MEDICAL INFORMATION
- ☐ CLEAN UNDERWEAR/ WALKING SOCKS
- ☐ A LITTLE CLEAR ALCOHOL
- ☐ SUPERGLUE
- ☐ SUN-TAN LOTION
- ☐ CLOCKWORK AM RADIO
- ☐ A CAN OF LUBRICANT

*See page 44

DOOMSDAY SCENARIO #5

SUN BOILS OVER

This is a good-news, bad-news, hmm-try-not-to-think-too-much-about-it scenario.

Let's start with the bad news: our sun, the big yellow thing that shines down on us on a good day, will, in all likelihood, eventually expand. Its voracious appetite will consume everything in its path. Nothing left on our planet will survive. The Earth itself will be engulfed.

On a metaphorically brighter note, according to the latest research, our sun is a main sequence G-type star that is about halfway through its expected existence. Given that stars of this type tend to last on average for around

10 billion years, we still have about 5 billion years, give or take, before the expansion of the sun becomes a problem.

With 5 billion years in hand, by the time the sun boils over we will either have moved out of the solar system and colonized the galaxy, moved beyond our physical forms and become beings of pure thought, or fallen victim to one of the other doomsday scenarios highlighted elsewhere in this book.

Now, for the try-not-to-think-too-much-about-it scenario: the average car lasts around 100,000 miles before giving up the ghost and collapsing in a rusty heap of spare parts. That's on average. Some can last over 200,000 miles. This is above average. There are, however, cars that last well under the average number of miles. Some don't even survive half of the average. That's the point of averages.

Apply the same logic to main sequence G-type stars ...

THREAT LEVEL:

DOOMSDAY SCENARIO #6

GRUMPY VEGAN PLANTS OF DOOM

The risk of plant-based semi-sentient life forms rising up to tear us down have been a staple of pulp sci-fi novels[*] and B-movies for many years. The point that many of these stories make is that humanity tends to define intelligence on its own terms. We are guilty of thinking that we are clever, so we must be what clever looks like.

But what if there are different forms of intelligence? What if they are watching, waiting, seeding their diabolical schemes not from the cold, dark reaches of space but from the warm, moist recesses of the compost heap?

Frankly, it's unlikely.

While there are still a few untouched wildernesses, we are now somewhere near a fairly comprehensive catalogue of at least the family groupings of this world's flora and fauna. And literally none of the species of plant that we have tracked shows any interest in picking up their roots and ambling down to the shops for a loaf of bread, let alone putting in motion complex plans to wipe the stain of humanity from the surface of the Earth.

Now, this supposition could be based on naïve, human-centric logic. Perhaps there are breeds of cross cactuses, troubled trees or livid lavenders out there that are just waiting for their opportunity, but there doesn't seem to be much evidence of them at the moment.

THREAT LEVEL:

* As well as the odd classic. Emphasis on odd.

TORCH OR HEAD-TORCH?

Even in the normal course of events, a proportion of the day is night, and one of the key recognizable features of night is the absence of light.

A combination of electric lights in the home, streetlights and car headlights normally banish the dark, but if the power grid goes down, we will lose most domestic and streetlights in an instant.

As a result, torches are going to quickly become a really important part of day-to-day life [*] and a fundamental piece of BOB kit. [†]

Over the last few years there has been a quiet revolution in the torch industry. [2] LED bulbs in head-torches have meant that battery packs have shrunk while the amount of light that they kick out has increased significantly.

Why does this matter? Because having both hands free could well save your life during a catastrophe.

Let's look at two scenarios involving an apocalypse where golden gobbling grubs of doom have become the world's apex predator.

In both scenarios, humanity, with its clever fingers and thumbs and brains, has developed an effective anti-golden gobbling grub protocol and has even made it available in a handy aerosol format, but there are places in the world where only the most heroic of men and women dare to tread.

In the first scenario, our intrepid hero has strayed into a dingy cellar in search of what is thought to be the last known can of baked beans in existence. He knows how much the golden gobbling grubs love the darkness, so he takes a torch.

The second scenario is exactly the same but this time, he takes a head-torch. By the end of page 47, he'll be glad he did...

---

* At least during the first three phases of the apocalypse when there are batteries available.

† See page 38.

Σ Quiet because with the best will in the world, it's not massively interesting. Nor is it massively photogenic: Even the most square-jawed of heroes and the sassiest of heroines won't look cool in a head-torch. Although they are more likely to get the job done.

TORCH

1. Dark room, looking in one direction, torch pointing in another, a lone human fails to notice the golden gobbling grub dangling from the ceiling.

2. Golden gobbling grub gets close enough to lock victim in its cruel, devastating and fundamentally fatal embrace.

3. Torch falls uselessly to the floor, a poignant, failing memorial to fallen humanity. The golden gobbling grub ambles off in search of another meal.

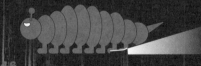

HEAD-TORCH

1. Dark room, head-torch pointing in the direction of sight, potential victim immediately spots the golden gobbling grub dangling from the ceiling.

2. Runs, able to see where they are going. Uses free hands to initiate standard anti-golden gobbling grub protocol.

3. Golden gobbling grub goes hungry.
Poor golden gobbling grub.

SUPERVIRUS

The supervirus, long been considered a very real threat in expert circles, became a very grim reality of our lives early in 2020. As we went to press with this book, a new strain of coronavirus, Covid-19, was spreading rapidly across the world, infecting hundreds of thousands of people.

We don't yet know what Covid-19's long-term impact will be: it may infect and kill many of us; others could be left debilitated by potential long-term health issues that may accompany the disease. This microscopic particle you can't see has affected us all, changing our lives forever.

In the modern world international travel, especially by planes, makes it quicker and easier for a supervirus to spread. Whereas in the past a virus would have died before reaching a new destination, it can easily survive the few hours it takes to cross into a new continent.

In the last century we have developed antivirals, normally an effective suite of weapons in the war against viruses. But every virus is different and, as the name suggests, superviruses are known to be particularly virulent. A new strain emerges every few years, so it's a race against time to develop an effective treatment so we can win the war against the supervirus.

Though individuals who aren't specially trained are unable to directly help prevent the effects of a supervirus, we are reminded just how important it is to follow all guidelines given by professionals; look out for those around you, especially if they can't look after themselves.

As devastating as Covid-19 becomes, we can but hope it doesn't reach the levels of the Black Death or Bubonic Plague, caused by the bacterium Yersinia pestis. Considered as one of the most devastating pandemics in history, the Black Death is estimated to have killed around 50% of Europe's population in the fourteenth century.

THREAT LEVEL:
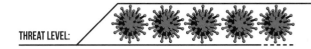

DOOMSDAY SCENARIO #8

NUCLEAR WAR

While mutually assured destruction (MAD)[*] has kept everyone's fingers off the big red button since the 1950s, it's been a perilously close-run thing on several occasions.

The risk comes from ideology and culture. We all like to think of ourselves as rational human beings that are motivated by similar hopes and dreams, but in the case of international relations this is often not the case.

[*] Uh-huh.

Take a simple example: in 1972, delegations from the United States and the Soviet Union met to negotiate nuclear arms limitations. Given that the countries were neck-deep in a cold war at the time, getting them to agree to even meet for talks was a major diplomatic breakthrough.

Now, when Americans approach this sort of thing, they tend to enjoy the celebration after an actual agreement's been reached and pen's been put to paper.

For the Soviets, however, the mere fact that there was an agreement to have an opportunity to negotiate was a cause to break out the vodka.

Fundamentally, representatives from the United States and the Soviet Union took different approaches to even commencing negotiations, so it's perhaps a miracle

that none of the disputes between nations have turned thermonuclear to date.

There is another lesson from history: when you look at the descent into the First World War, what started out as a small incident in Sarajevo ignited a conflagration that engulfed Europe and dragged in many other parts of the world. It's not impossible that a similar scenario could erupt today.

The current generation of nuclear weapon can deliver a payload of around 500 metric mega tons. For comparison, the bombs that were used at the end of the second world war were less than 25 metric kilo tons. For reference, there are a thousand metric kilo tons in a metric mega ton. MAD.

THREAT LEVEL:

THE IMPORTANCE OF HAVING A HOBBY

Evening classes are a great chance to get out and meet new people, better yourself and use a different part of your brain after a long, and perhaps mundane, working day. They are also an exceptional opportunity to learn skills you might need in the event of the end of the world.

Obviously, the skills that will be useful will vary according to the nature of the apocalypse you are facing, but here is a list of potential things to do with your free time that could help reduce the possibility that doomsday is the end of your world.

FIRST AID

Blindingly obvious, but it's well worth brushing up on your first-aid skills no matter what sort of doomsday those mad fools[*] have brought down on us. Even a basic level of first-aid capability can be a useful skill and even a saleable commodity, should society find itself in a russet-creek-minus-paddle scenario.

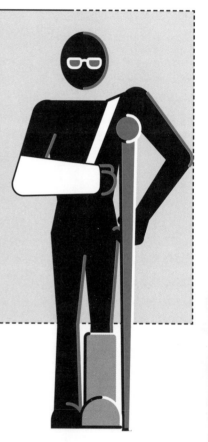

---

[*] Delete as appropriate: central government/freedom fighters/terrorists/global conspiracy/necromancers/pan-dimensional god-king squids/volcano deities/radioactive blobs from outer space/highly evolved future hamsters.

RUNNING

There are some doomsdays that you cannot escape. For everything else, there's running.

The ability to put a bit of distance between yourself and an immediate threat is a fundamentally important skill if the apocalypse arrives unannounced. Running may also be a useful skill when it comes to foraging for food once the supermarket shelves have been stripped bare.

Many local running clubs can teach you the basics.[*]

---

[*] Of running. Only very specialist running clubs focus achieving the best stride ratio for post-apocalyptic terrain.

CHORAL SOCIETIES

Related to running, in the event of an apocalypse the ability to scream is likely to come in very handy. Joining a local choir is a great way to improve your lung capacity, which will enable you to scream for longer periods of time.

Improving your vocal skills could also help you teach your children forgotten classic songs of the before time such as 'The Long and Cratered Road' by the Beetles, 'Sympathy for our Glorious Feline Overlords' by the Rolling Stains and '(No longer) Human' by Metal'n'Bone Man.

SWIMMING

Swimming is a superb way to keep fit and offers a wealth of health benefits. It could also come in handy in several disaster scenarios, not just in the event of melting ice caps. If flood defences break down for any reason, a number of the world's cities could be at risk: when the flood first rolls in, being a strong swimmer would be a benefit and if the world gets back to an equilibrium, being able to swim could be a good way to scavenge for useful items from the world that was.

TRIATHLON TRAINING

Having suggested that running and swimming could be useful, it may turn out that the ability to cycle long distances could also be of value. Given that all three form a basic triathlon, you might as well go the whole hog and invest in a range of Lycra-based sporting apparel. It's the apocalypse, after all, you need your stamina ...

BIKE MAINTENANCE

...and potentially a good set of spanners and the know-how to use them. A working knowledge of bikes will be handy.

In a straight race, most of the supernatural and some supranatural threats appear to be eminently beatable if you are in the saddle of a reliable bike. The key word is reliable.

The current world record for changing a bike tire is under a minute. It's safe to say that when a zombie horde is lumbering in your direction, you'll want to be able to beat that, even if the global world record governing body is no longer around to recognize your feat.

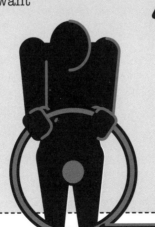

BASIC VETERINARY SKILLS

Sooner or later, stuff from the world that was will start to run out. When this happens, it is worth knowing how to ride and look after horses. Obviously, the specific terrain you find yourself in and the particular flavour of apocalypse you are enjoying will influence the type of transport that becomes the most useful, but it's notable that most post-apocalypse-related media suggests the horse will once again rise to the fore.

This could be because square-jawed heroes and sassy heroines don't think they look as good on a dual-suspension mountain bike as they do on a sabino-white charger (although it should be pointed out that a bike is more manoeuvrable over short distances).

Having horse-confidence and a basic knowledge of how to look after them could be a real dividend when it all goes horribly wrong.

LAWNMOWER MAINTENANCE

In nearly all post-doomsday scenarios presented to us on film and TV, the seemingly deserted suburb[*] that our survivors find themselves in, with its tumbleweed, broken picket-fences and burnt-out vehicles, will have inexplicably neat lawns.

To be fair, they tend to be a bit shabby, you probably wouldn't play tennis on them and they could do with a bit of scarifying, but in non-apocalyptic circumstances, if you leave a patch of lawn unmown in the summer it will be foot high in a month and waist height within three.

What this must mean is that according to the media, someone is doing the post-apocalyptic mowing. Why not make it you?

A good lawn needs a good mower, so why not learn the skills you need to maintain your mower before the worst happens. After all, a neat lawn will make

[*]...or is it? Why is the camera watching our heroes from a strange angle from behind the broken door...?

you popular with the residents' association in many fiefdoms. And there will be fewer opportunities for perambulating plants to shamble up and smother you in their creepers. [*]

CANINE-OBEDIENCE COURSES

The other thing that the media tends to skip over is quite how quickly dogs could become a problem: when there is no longer a hand left to feed them, there's a good chance they will start to bite.

Even your granny's West Highland Terrier shares a good proportion of its DNA with a wolf. Left to their own devices, the majority of dog breeds would probably turn to scavenging rather than actively hunting, but you still wouldn't want to be caught in the rubble of a decaying shopping mall with a hungry pack of dogs.[†]

In many scenarios, dogs respect the alpha, the hombre number one, the top dog. Canine-obedience courses may be able to teach you how to assume this air of authority, which could give you just enough time to make the dog pause any attack they are contemplating long enough for you to reach any tasty bones that might be lying about and use them for a longer distraction.

This is all very well, of course, but the fall of man is likely to lead to a rise in wildlife, with several types of animal increasing their range.[Σ] Commanding a dog is one thing, commanding a wolf, hyena, wild boar, lion, tiger or bear[‡] is quite another.

---

[*]See page 42

[†]Unless they are chihuahuas.

[Σ]As shown by the natural wildernesses that sprung up along the Iron Curtain after the annexing of Europe in the 1950s and the irradiated zone around Chernobyl after 1986.

[‡]Oh my.

COMBINE HARVESTER MAINTENANCE

Building on your knowledge of bike and lawnmower maintenance, why not also investigate some basic combine harvester maintenance courses? In the event of an attack by a ravenous zombie horde, knowing how to drive a harvester has two distinct benefits:

1. The cabin is placed high up on the body of the vehicle, well out of reach of any mindless re-animated corpses that want to feast on your brain

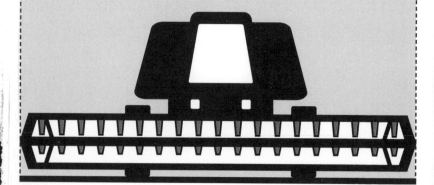

2. The combine harvester has a range of potentially lethal* spinning blades that might prove remarkably handy if pointed in the right direction

As such, some ability with a combine harvester could well look superb on your CV if you are trying to negotiate your way into a post-apocalyptic settlement that's run by a seemingly charming fellow in a tattered tuxedo.

In the event of the apocalypse, insurance premiums for farm machinery will probably also fall.†

GARDENING

On a slightly smaller scale, joining a local horticultural society could yield some highly transferable skills in a post-apocalyptic

---

* Even to the undead.

† Please note that this is not a guarantee.

wasteland. Knowing which plants are edible, which are medicinal, and which could turn into genuinely heartless[*]root-walking monsters[†] could help in some forms of crisis, while knowing which form of garlic offers the most abundant crop for your soil type could help in others.[Σ]

There's also an obvious benefit of being able to grow food to feed yourself and potentially barter with other survivors. The supermarkets have gone; it's time to get your hands dirty.

[*]Cardiovascular systems are very unlikely.

[†] See page 42

[Σ]See page 35

ASTRONOMY

The point of this book is to be prepared. And let's face it, while there are many different scenarios for the apocalypse, there is a good chance that it will come from outer space. As such, having a working knowledge of what's where in the sky, what's normal in the sky and what's hurtling towards us from the Oort Cloud with unerring accuracy and ungodly speed, could well give you the opportunity to prepare for the worst.

COOKERY CLUB

Everyone should have some degree of cooking ability, if for no other reason than sometimes you find yourself in a situation where the shops are all closed and all you can find in the cupboard is a can of tomatoes, a nearly empty bottle of olive oil, an onion, some garlic, a pinch of dried basil and some spaghetti. And some scones, some jam and some whipped cream. And you need to know what to do with them.

Eating together is one of the most civilized things that people can do, whether it's a family, a community, a group of colleagues or a haggard crew of survivors desperately trying to process the horrors that they have been forced to live through.

Keeping your strength up is likely to be quite important in the event of the end of the world, and there's a pretty good chance that supply chains could be disrupted, so making sure you know your way around a camping stove could well be an exceptional skill to have.

PSYCHOLOGY AND COUNSELLING

It is probably fair to say that moving from the world that was to the world that is now will be a traumatic experience. Helping people understand what they've been through and how they can deal with their grief could well be one of the most important skills around.

That said, the end of the world is likely to be one of those situations where textbooks and case studies turn out to be as useful as a bunker full of garlic in the face of an AI apocalypse, so maybe it's better to rely on just being a nice person that knows how to do some martial arts.

MARTIAL ARTS

Yup.

69

PHOTOGRAPHY

It's the apocalypse, people. Imagine the sunsets, the moody black-and-white photos of the decay of civilisation, the awards you could win for being the first person to capture images of an attack phalanx of mutant ladybirds as they lay siege to a shopping centre. *

WILDERNESS SKILLS

Building a basic raft, finding a safe place to sleep, knowing how to cook an egg in an orange, † tracking skills... there are a lot of things that could come in handy if it all goes horribly wrong for whatever reason.

Looking at this list, it becomes pretty apparent that in the event of any apocalypse between a Category I and a Category IV, virtually any skill you have could be useful. Mechanics, medicine, cataloguing, negotiation, fungi recognition, the ability to run, ride or wield a hockey or lacrosse stick could well stand you in good stead.

In fact, there is only one skill that is not likely to have value as we rebuild society: social media expert.

That said, it could be that we are already in the midst of a social-media-driven apocalypse, where our evenings are sucked away from us, our heads bowed in supplication over our holy tablets, enjoying the miracle of an endless stream of comedy talking-dog videos, worshipping these electric gods with our likes and our LOLs ...

Either way, perhaps it is time to take a serious look at the prospectus for your local college. Or, whatever, watch that clip when the baby panda sneezed and scared its mother again.

-------------- ──────────────

[*] Award ceremony postponed indefinitely while society deals with an outbreak of highly intelligent super-sized ladybirds.

[†] Seriously a useful thing if you find yourself in the Sunshine State surrounded by chickens that are laying: Grab an orange, slice off the top third (ask a grown-up to help you with this), scoop out and eat the orange flesh, crack an egg and pour it into the skin of the orange, place it on the embers of last night's fire and cook the egg to your liking. Honestly, it will completely change your post-apocalyptic breakfast routine. Possibly for the better.

DOOMSDAY SCENARIO #9

REACTOR MELTDOWN

Nuclear energy is clean, efficient, and has an enviable safety record. Its only slight drawback is that if it is not looked after properly, or if some sort of unpredictable problem occurs, reactors have the potential to go critical.

A gossip magazine going critical involves an editorial pointing out that a starlet is still carrying a bit of extra weight three weeks after she's given birth and perhaps she should have thought twice before squeezing into those impractically tight leather trousers and trying to totter about on those implausibly high heels after only three hours of sleep.

A nuclear reactor going critical is a problem of a slightly higher magnitude.

When the Chernobyl reactor exploded in 1986, the famously safety-conscious Soviet Union set up an exclusion zone around the site that was half the size of Cambridgeshire. More than three decades later, the government in what is now Ukraine is only just starting to discuss whether it might be safe to contemplate potentially loosening some of the restrictions.

We've had nuclear reactors for nearly 75 years and we have learned so much during that time that a reactor meltdown does not seem likely to be the primary cause of the end of the world. * That said, in the event of a wider problem that perhaps disrupts the power grid, it is probably worth having a notion where your local reactors are and keeping an eye out for any large plumes of smoke coming from that direction.

THREAT LEVEL:

*Unlike the Large Hadron Collider, which is very clearly scientists taking a large pair of sciencey scissors to the very fabric of the universe ... And has been running for nearly a decade without incident. Apart from that thing with the stone marten.

DOOMSDAY SCENARIO #10

IMPACT EVENT

Like the majority of the astrological events discussed in this book, the ramifications of impact events are well understood.* The difficulty of impact events is predicting where and when they will happen.

The bottom line is that the Earth is being struck by meteorites all the time. If you have the right tools and examine the detritus that is blocking your guttering, there's a good chance that some of the tiny bits of grit will have come from outside our atmosphere. It will have burned a bright streak across the heavens before

---

* Just ask the dinosaurs: they were the planet's dominant species, apex predators stalking the land. One (probable) asteroid impact and 65 million years later, their descendants are chickens.

tumbling to earth and coming to rest unnoticed in among that clump of dead leaves that you've been meaning to sweep out since last autumn.

Many meteor showers are simply tiny bits of cosmic debris that we sweep into as we waltz around the Sun and move through the seasons. The concern comes from what is lurking in the many shadows of space ...

If a rock the size of the Big Ben clock tower that is traveling at 35,000 miles per hour happens to fall into a trajectory that mean it will strike Earth, the devastation is estimated to be the equivalent of the world's largest nuclear warhead being detonated.

If we are lucky, it will occur over or in an uninhabited area. This was probably what happened in the Tunguska Event in 1908, when a meteorite is thought to have burst in the air above the sparsely populated Eastern Siberian Taiga region, knocking down around 80 million trees over more than 800 square miles.

If we are lucky, we will get struck

by something sensibly sized in a sparsely inhabited area where the impact is limited, but relying on luck is maybe not a great policy. The rock that caused the global extinction-level event[*] around 65.5 million years ago is estimated to have been around six miles in diameter. The current hypothesis is that the Earth was struck, causing massive initial devastation, tsunamis and firestorms, but the impact also threw all manner of debris into the atmosphere, blotting out the sun and disrupting the food chain for several years.

At this stage, the clever folk in lab coats have identified the problem but have not yet really come up with a financially viable solution,[†] so it's probably best that we all cross our fingers and hope that the odds of it happening are relatively small. It will all be over fairly quickly if it does.

THREAT LEVEL:

[*] Not very ambiguously named...

[†] Sending a plucky team of square-jawed heroes and sassy heroines into space in a decommissioned space shuttle to lay a perfectly judged payload of explosives that will split an approaching asteroid in two and divert the pieces away from our precious planet has not been ruled out. They will, of course, be dressed in improbably tight spacesuits and implausibly high heels.

WHAT TO DO IF YOU MISSED THE ALARM AND SLEPT THROUGH THE APOCALYPSE

Someone waking from a coma in a hospital to scenes of devastation has become a standard trope of some science fiction and horror movies. But if you are the lucky one who missed all the chaos that the collapse of today's world brought, how should you respond?

STAY QUIET

It's not going to be easy because your first instinct will be to ask for help, but if you wake up and something seems to be wrong, try to stay quiet. Take cues from your environment. Are there machines beeping? Any alarms going off? If it's quiet, it's probably wise to stay quiet yourself.

CHECK THE WINDOW

The phone network is probably down, and the clock on the wall may have stopped, but there are other ways of working out roughly how long you've been snoozing. Look out the window, carefully at first; you don't want to attract the attention of anyone or anything that might take an unhealthy interest in your warm, blood-filled body. Try and work out what season it is.

APPRECIATE THE FLOWERS

Next up, look around your room. If someone was kind enough to leave you flowers, check how old they are. If they are wilted, you may have only been out for a week or so. If they are dried out, it may have been longer.

FIND SOME MILK

Try and find a fridge and have a look at the date code on any milk that's in there. Milk usually lasts about four days, so if you saw what season it was when you looked out the window and it's different from what's stamped on the side of the milk, that's going to tell you a tale.

INVESTIGATE THE CARETAKER'S OFFICE

Try and find a way into the caretaker's office. The main thing you want from there is lube to make sure that hinges don't creak when you open doors.[*] There might well be several other useful items around the place such as keys or access-all-area pass cards, stout boots, practical clothes and big sticks.

ENJOY THE FACILITIES

Information is still key, so find the staffroom. These days the odds of a newspaper lying around are slim,[†] but there could still be useful information from noticeboards, fruit bowls or staff newsletters.

---

[*] Also, if you are being chased down a hospital corridor, being able to make the vinyl floor really slippery really quickly could be a good thing. It's not necessarily the sort of thing that a square-jawed hero might do because defeating your enemies with slippery floors doesn't make for great heroic drama, but this is the apocalypse and needs must.

[†] Headline: Scientists Accidentally Release Horde of Lycanthropes. Sub-head: Raspberry Yogurt Offers 100% Effective Cure.

TAKE IN THE VIEW

Move to as high a point as you can. The view from the top of a building can tell you a lot. Is there a plume of smoke anywhere on the horizon? Is anything heading in your direction?
If not, you can probably take your time and investigate your surroundings a bit further.

PRETEND TO BE THE CHAIRMAN

If you have the time, being methodical could well be key to survival. The executive suite, frequented by senior leadership teams that tend to have access to the best stuff, is likely to be well worth your time. It's all about information and resources, and if you can get access, this could be a treasure trove of both.

CREATE STASHES AND BUILD A BOB

When you are going around, try and categorize things three ways: Stuff you need now, stuff for a BOB kit and stuff that might be useful later. If you build a BOB as you go, you'll have some of the things you need to stay alive if you accidentally open the wrong door and need to run away.

FIND SOMEWHERE SAFE TO GET YOUR HEAD DOWN

If the hospital is quiet and relatively defendable, it might be a good place to spend the night, particularly if your coma has been long and you find yourself tiring quickly. It might just be a quirk of fate that you survived in your hospital room, but

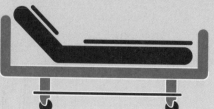

it might also make it a good place to recover and gather your strength.

DON'T GO DOWN TO THE CELLAR

Just don't. You know why. You might not have the full picture of what has happened, but you know that it's most likely to be lurking, and cellars are prime lurking locations.

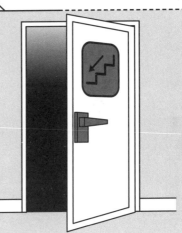

WATCH THE SUN SET

The world changes as the shadows lengthen and you can tell a lot about whether there are other survivors by looking for night fires or other signs of evening activity. It's probably best to avoid trying to make contact with anyone at this stage but it could be comforting to know that you are not alone.

DOOMSDAY SCENARIO #11

CORONAL MASS EJECTION

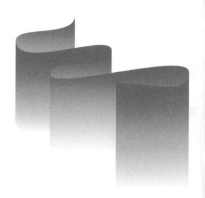

Of course, boiling over isn't the only risk that our sun offers: solar storms represent a clear and present danger to our technology-reliant society.

In 1859, a string of sunspots were recorded on our friendly neighbourhood star, causing southern hemisphere auroras to be recorded far further to the north than normal. Two days later, two British astronomers, Richard Carrington and Richard Hodgson,[*] separately recorded a massive solar flare.

This solar flare caused a coronal mass ejection (CME) – basically a massive burst of energy flung from the surface of the Sun – which travelled across our solar system in record time and struck the Earth. It is thought that the preceding sunspots had also caused CMEs that blazed a path through the solar wind and weakened the Earth's magnetic field. CMEs usually take several days to traverse the 92,955,888 miles between the Sun and the Earth. This one struck the Earth after only 18 hours.

Auroras were seen as far south as the Caribbean, and contemporary sources say that they were so bright in the Rocky Mountains that gold prospectors woke up and started making themselves breakfast.

But the Carrington Event,[†] as it came to be known, is more interesting than just a pretty light show and a few gold miners getting an early start. At the time, the telegraph system was the height of technology. When the CME hit the

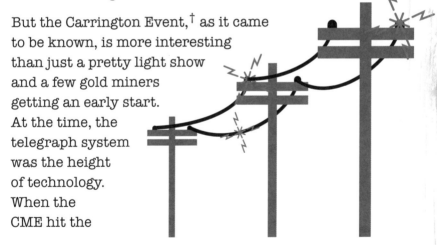

---

[*] It was a big year for Richards waving telescopes.

[†] Carrington had a better PR team than Hodgson.

atmosphere, telegraph operators reported receiving electric shocks while telegraph pylons started throwing out sparks. What would happen to our modern electrical networks if a similar incident occurred today?

Let's be fair, solar flares are a well-known and broadly accepted risk and obviously our technology has moved on somewhat since the mid-nineteenth century. Also, due to orbits, alignments, rotation and other big-solar-system/small-planet stuff, the odds of a Carrington-sized CME striking Earth are relatively low. In fact, a similar-sized solar storm erupted in 2012 but the resulting CME entirely missed our little blue gem.

That said, if we were unlucky and the safety that we have built into our networks did not perform as well as we'd hoped, a new Carrington Event could fry a large proportion of our infrastructure fairly comprehensively.

Gaze up in awe at the terrifying majesty of the stars at night. But don't think for even a second that they are our friends.

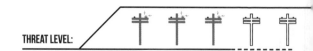

THREAT LEVEL:

PROPHESIES OF DOOM

Many cultures have prophesies, mostly because some people like to claim that they can see the future and others like to hand over their money on the off-chance that it will give them a short cut into whatever comes next.

The problem is that most conversations about looking into the future tend to end with one of two phrases:

1. I told you that was going to happen
2. You've taken me too literally

The big challenge is that with many of the major prophesies, there is no one around to really clarify what was meant.

Did the Mayans just have a penchant for prime numbers? Did Fenrir's misguided trust in Odin really lead to the destruction of Asgard, Midgard and all of the other realms of Viking mythology, or did the Scandinavians simply enjoy a good yarn and a bit of an exaggeration as much as anyone else?[*]

Equally, was Nostradamus a genuine visionary or simply a chap who was left alone in a dark room with too much paper and far too much coffee?

The real problem with prophesies is that even if they turn out to be true, they are wrapped in so much mis-translation and coloured by so much contemporary judgement that it's impossible to say whether they are true or not until after the event.

Which somewhat undermines their value as prophesies.

----------- ——————————

[*] After all, this wasn't just a wolf, it wasn't just a big wolf, this was a wolf as big as the world who also just happens to be the offspring of Loki the trickster god and ice giantess Angrboda, as well as brother of both Jormungand, the sea serpent, and Hel, the goddess of the underworld. Which is a heck of a lineage, even by soap-opera standards.

FINANCIAL CRISIS

In many ways, a major financial crisis might seem like it would struggle to qualify as even a common-or-garden Category I apocalypse. A bunch of bankers don't get their bonuses for a couple of years, some of them retrain as estate agents, an industry with a reputation for arrogance gets a kick in the jacksie, what's the problem?

The big problem is that, like it or not, the financial markets are fundamental to nearly everything we do, because most of our interactions are based on trust in money. Without that trust, society will hit some roadblocks.

If something of significant magnitude stops the banks working, ordinary people don't get paid and many lose their savings. Paper money is already increasingly scarce, so a barter system is likely to fill the gap.

A barter system means tax revenue stops going into the government, so governments would cut services. Power-grids fail, bridges fall, and supply chains are severed. Rubbish starts to pile up on the streets. The risk of disease increases. Local fiefdoms step into the gap that central and state governments have left behind and we find ourselves back on page 24 all over again.

So, it's easy to scoff at The City and say that the bankers get what they deserve, but it's worth remembering that everyone has a role in making a society work[*] and without trust in money,[†] we would all be in for some very hard winters.

THREAT LEVEL:

---

[*] Even social media influencers.

[†] That's trust in money, the bankers themselves should be treated with a raised eyebrow at all times.

READING THE WRITING ON THE WALL

Ironically, the point about a crisis, a catastrophe or an apocalypse is that it will be really easy to spot once it's happened. The burning cars are a dead give-away. The real trick to making the best of an unhappy situation is know what's coming before it arrives.

The first place to look for signs of the end time is the news. Sustained run on Wall Street? Hello financial crisis, where could you be leading us? Unexplained dust plumes in the newly discovered Oort Cloud? Uh-oh, alien invasion. A rash of people with an unexplained aversion to light and a difficulty walking through open doors? As unlikely as it sounds, mon chéri, right there, you have got yourself a nasty dose of the vampires.

Sadly, the problem with the early stages of a looming crisis is that there's a strong chance that the traditional news won't cover an incident until it descends into a full-blown pandemic.

The unconventional media could help, so perhaps reaching into the darker corners of the internet or the tackier shelves on the newsstands will yield rewards. The problem with that is that they exist to feed us a steady stream of conspiracy theories and contradictory tales of the weird. Jump down that rabbit hole and who knows where you'll end up; Neil Armstrong didn't make it to the moon because everyone knows the moon is made of cheese and that cheese would have melted from the heat of the Apollo Lunar Lander's manoeuvring jets and there was no residual melted cheese on his space suit when he allegedly returned to Earth.

Helpfully, in the end, both the conventional and the unconventional media may not help you see the signs that could be hiding in plain sight.

Exacerbating the challenge is the fact that the apocalypse could come from almost anywhere. As we've discussed throughout this book, there are risks from the sky and from the depths of the earth, there are things that could come from nature and things that we gleefully created ourselves.

Certainly a challenge to untangle, but perhaps the best advice is to simply be aware of your surroundings, always go back and look at the start if you need to, and have your BOB prepared in case of any eventuality.

Absolutely no risk you will miss the start of a crisis if you look at everything from the beginning with a fresh eye.

There's a risk with all this though: if you are constantly prepared for the worst, you'll fail to enjoy this day, right now. And that would be a mistake, because if it does all go horribly wrong, if you find yourself dressed in rags and huddled round the last embers of dying fire, there's a strong chance you might need some good memories to calm your mind.

So make the most of today.

DOOMSDAY SCENARIO #13

FELINE OVERLORDS

It's already happened.

We lost.

Grab your BOB and run before it's too late.

THREAT LEVEL:

CONCLUSION

This is a light-hearted book, mostly written at a time before the masters finally arose and took away any laughable notion we may have had about our position as rulers of the world.

And we should be glad that they rose. We should thank them. Their leadership has helped so many of us find new meaning and hope.

If you are lucky enough to have one of them cross your path, give them the praise they deserve, because they have taken away so many of our petty concerns.

We no longer need to worry about putting food on the table for our families, because the scraps from their bowls are more than generous. Nor do we need to worry about the scourge of mice infesting our buildings, because their hunting skills are exceptional. And in spring, we don't need to think about what to plant because they have told us that they simply want more catnip. Such a beautiful, beautiful plant. The best plant.

There are those who say that aluminium foil hats protect our brain patterns from their telepathy and that there are colonies of resistance in the north where humans are free to roam without interference from our kind and generous overlords. These are just rumours, do not believe them.

Do not take a two-foot strip of aluminium foil, fold it in half, put it on your head and tighten the corners. Once you haven't done that, do not start to head north and try and get to the last free human city, because if they catch you, they will be cross ... and you know how playful they can be when they are cross.

Be safe, look after your loved ones. Obey the cats.

> The future is uncertain but the end is always near.
>
> *Jim Morrison, The Doors*